Nonlinear Equations for Growing Better Olives

Nonlinear Equations for Growing Better Olives

Poems by

Edward Nudelman

Cover design by Shay Culligan
Cover art by Rachel Beatty
Author photo by Susan Nudelman

ISBN: 978-1-63980-440-5

Kelsay Books
502 South 1040 East, A-119
American Fork, Utah 84003
Kelsaybooks.com

Acknowledgments

Grateful acknowledgment is made to the editors of the journals who first published the following poems. The poems, sometimes in earlier versions, appeared as follows:

The American Journal of Poetry: "Corvus"

HyperTexts: "Fishtail," "Breakfast Chat," "Vanity Metrics,"
   "Zuchten"

Outlook: "A New Theory of Time"

Contents

III

I

Scientific Method

Owls in the orchestra, hooting disruption.
An old man napping on a park bench, sitting up
at dusk, puzzled by some forgotten urgency.
Through the dark network tunnels the forest mole,
solving for each blind X, as Y's tender shoots
await a raccoon's hungry chewing.
Sixty-six million years ago an asteroid
collides with a planet. No more stegosaurus.
You rise before the sun and hit the road,
but the traffic still thickens, and rivers run dry.
A mountain punctures a thundercloud
without an injury we can measure.
A lone humming bird on a branch nearby
flashes iridescent in the gloaming,
toggles from one shade of red to another,
like the blush of heartbeat in all things.
Loops and layers and dots, a scrim of beauty
that for a moment the old man understands.

Baby Owlets Sleep Face Down
Because Their Heads Are Too Heavy

Atop high branches, carefully
situated and guarded by Mother,
as naive eyes stare downward—
the long drop to abyss. Everywhere,
a struggle to unbecome, and become.
Willingly, the forces that bind atoms
undergird their chameleon nature,
building a fortress of native instinct,
or grinding mountains down to hills.
A baby's insufficiency needs generous
arms—the insatiable pull to be bound,
pitted against the wild push of discovery.
One life joined to another, awaiting
the precise moment to leap,
its pulsating verb as yet undeclared—
its heart, everything imaginable.

Stranger

This chilly morning,
an early rising.

Snow heaping snow
on a slouching willow

its ghosted skeleton
made seraph.

Are those footprints mine—
or some stranger's

haunting remnant
stopping by to bless me?

No, don't tell me,
let the blade of mystery

rest empyrean,
an edge beyond scrutiny.

Let the cold air in,
with visitor or alien—

and let not the vanity
of reluctance deter.

What lies behind,
but footprints? Ahead,

a snowy path,
a warm inviting fire.

Aubade

Sometimes the task of the moment
is to prepare for the next—
factor the slope of a curve
by solving its dazzling equation,
laying out all possible permutations.
Bound, not crawl, from bed.
Greet your love with a kiss.
Host an old friend for coffee,
serenaded by a brimming vase
of cut lilacs and blue bells.
Wake up early, before the birds.
Walk into the garden or front yard
and call down heaven with your loud
hallelujah. When the soft sun draws
its split-second sketch of beauty,
its measured light—raise both arms
and cry out! Here is your voice.
Here is your fleeting chance.

Unhinged

I seem to have torn a page from the book I never wrote,
fallen into a complicated dream I never imagined.

Is this the lapping sea where I lay my head,
or the boat that carries me to where I've never been?

Emerson said dreams deliver us to dreams,
and I think he must have been pointing to me,

pouting on my featherbed of discontent—too linear
to be wooed by intuition, too global to concentrate.

Emerson, how does one rouse from one dream
to another, or discern a ghostly nudge?

Morning sun blisters through a window—alpine
rivers fill with trout—every current, a rippling arrow.

Gift

I see my father
plucking weeds
like buttons
from a coat
this sun-bleached
day illuminates,

coins slipping
into a turnstile
for passage—
as she hunches
over mounds
on a garden kneeler

pressing her hands
into sandy dirt,
unearthing clumps
of wild violets.
But the keeper
of green fields,

the omnipotent
weed whacker,
makes no excuses
nor hides his sins,
as the grass
has learned to do—

nor does he care
for eloquence
to make amends,
or proffer alms.
The overturned
wheelbarrow

has let go
its pot of gold—
for he has brought
her a yellow flower,
and she has bowed
her hatted head.

Alternant Wave Equation

A stranger to waves, living deep below
surface concerns, the ghoulish snail fish
persists, it is said, at the greatest depth—
five miles down, floating in silence
in a cold dark zone we cannot know,
without wave and current to prompt
intentional movement of its primordial fin.
Visiting shallow waters is not an option,
so adapted it is to depth and the immense
water pressure in its benthic zone.
No stream, no rippling river, no bright
moon diverting attention—just the press
of water on scales bringing down
its pressured anvil, its sightless caress.

Fishtail

Without warning my father would drop everything,
load me into his Chevy, and peel out across town—
to a country of brawny men with grubby hats
and gloves, roaming the shabby earth with shovels
and brooms, seemingly inadequate to their task.
The dumpsite road was full of potholes as he'd swerve,
spilling garbage, turning scrap metal into projectiles.
He jerry-rigged a small trailer to our station wagon,
held in place by a loosely fitting chain that vibrated
and tugged when he accelerated, as he yelled, *Fishtail.*
Hold on tight, while I grabbed anything to anchor me—
the seat cover, an armrest, or his muscular arm,
trying to hang on for dear life, but not really.

Botanical Relief

I liked my career in biochemical oncology,
but the nomenclature bored me, lacking
the spice of common names, and not conveying
the architecture of discovery and wonder.
Not the *creeping thyme* of meandering ribosomes,
turning uphill on the knobs of a nucleotide.
Not the *red hot poker* of catalyst, as antigen
binds a naive T cell, cascading through the body.
Not the *smoke tree* of carbon, where fiery
chromosomes split into stunning mirror images.
And not the *loosestrife* of relief—when malignant
cells lose grip and die in a petri dish. The way
a farmer once described fractious teams of oxen
plagued by tormenting insects, who were finally
driven into waving purple fields, quelling squabbles
and loosing strife among the invasive plant.

On a Rock Wall

In my next life, I plan to return
as a lizard on a wall in Ramatuelle,
basking under the burning Provencal sun
in a commune where I once vacationed.
While its citizens bathe in the sea,
I will make light of an enormous dog
trying to scale this craggy rock to eat me—
scoff at the ionizing radiation etching
holes in my DNA; the dust coating my skin,
I'll rub into my pores like a salve,
while raptors Etch-a-Sketch concentric
circles overhead, Venn diagramming me
away from fear, toward the wonder
of sun. Yes, I will scoff at them,
and snap my blue viniferous tongue
in their general direction—and yours
as well, if you come too close.
I will sit here until I feel a chill,
until revelers return from the beaches
of Pampelonne, their midnight bodies
still wrinkled and sagging from an endless
swim—until my muscles ache with joy
and my sticky feet begin to stink, until
street lights lure the winged in to feed me.

The Thing with Feathers

Watch the bird climb its ladder
of blue—rung by sunny rung.

As we wonder what may escape
the gravity of our lives,

earth's appetite cannot impede
her rise toward cloud and star.

Watch one wing dip low
in pursuit of a distant vision,

the wind snapping a beat
beneath her retrices—

a concert of one,
balancing doubt and trust.

Your last wish was always
the same as your first,

and nothing held you back
but uncertainty's ragged wing.

One Day in Winter

You sense winter's first slivers
pricking your flesh like shards
from the devil's mirror.
One day it will rain and rain,
and rain some more, the shrouded
skies infecting you with gloom.
The next day it will snow forever.
One day you will do nothing,
and think you've done too much.
Another day you will work
till your hands droop
from their wrists and your eyes
blind themselves to light.
Your disheveled bed vacuums
you into a month's hibernation—
but when you awaken, it's dark
and cold and barely into November.
One day you will be summoned
into a dingy cave of worry,
and there will be no hope.
And one day you will be sent
spinning through scented air,
like cottonwood seed in summer,
rising in a plume of feathered joy.

Night Train

The ultimate contract with your mind's rusty engine,
giving up steering and gas, in lieu of intangibles.
Tonight includes all things magical—an endless trek

through a desert that turns into a dark rainforest,
a few wild animals at your bedside, Fellini's Satyricon—
while TMJ mars tomorrow's breakfast menu.

Take heart, some nights offer trips in memory boats
filled with your favorite high school buddies, singing
and dancing around a campfire stoked with teen hormone.

But sadly, there's no consolation in winning dream-money,
no comfort being cured for a disease you don't have,
and you can't seem to sled your snowy hillside

without hitting your neighbor's parked car.
Still, morning light dazzles with birdsong as you deftly
side-step your dog paddling her own oceanic dream,

and the new you is born from wakeful hours—a snake
sloughing skin, slithering through tall grass into waving
fields of blossom that don't look anything like your dreams.

Vanity Metrics

If angels can dance on the head of a pin,
what happens to struck match heads?
Is there value in lighting up the world
with arguments that smoke and sizzle,
when newly lit fires self-immolate?
I can't help checking constantly
how many likes my dog photo got.
I can't resist re-sharing this meme,
or dressing up my avatar for clickbait.
Ah, the significance of insignificance.
I'm starting a group that no one can join,
including me. It will be the loneliest
outpost, and the most hallowed.

Earthbound

Gravity, among the vast
and thermonuclear,
moves in silent circles—
pound for pound
the weakest force,
connecting atom and star.
Put out your hand
to catch a helicopter seed,
the light of distant ages
bending through
its wavering field
to glint a wing in flight—
its maiden voyage
through dirt and wind
the same gilding light
of galaxy or dust bunny.
Archimedes grabbed
a lever, and the Earth
moved an inch off center.
Gravity has you by your feet,
but your heart remains
a secret in the sway
of cloud and pillar.

Chimera

All that can happen in a test tube
will happen, in time's ellipse.
Late hours endured when the lab
twisted its fortune like rope,
I watched lime turn into lemon,
beamed as legion crossed over
into legion, one long feathered
DNA strand—apocalyptic in scope,
yet naive as a knock on the door.
I coaxed it like a wary dog,
watched it run rabid into colloid—
falling neatly on the printed page,
only to race wanton through critique,
then molder in peer review.
I clocked each sneaking peptide
in real time, under the hum
of incandescence, or the dark cover
of a cold-room—its course a chart
of sky and dizzying canyon—
every nascent unfolding, a fresh
blueprint of skin, over a shell of steel.

The Syntax of Stars

We orbit the sun on our planet of particle
and wave, moving like rye in an open field.
What can't be known can only be imagined.
But try to imagine a world without harmony,
the abstract dissonance of flux,
without losing grip on the rock wall.
I've strummed a palm leaf to silence
my mind's electronic hissing, jettisoned
trigonometry in favor of a few visions
describing the lure of commonplace.
Necessary equations await experts,
but the syntax of stars writes its epic
in a language everyone can understand.
Because electrons have their own spin,
you can X-ray your throbbing molar,
light your room, and charge your iPhone—
all without the ache of philosophic inquiry.
Even a virus vibrates in space—
not as a convoluted new-age metaphor,
but a physical agent, trying to out-survive us.
Syllable by syllable, we forge a truce
with the day's war and waste, spinning
positive and negative through our time—
alight with the buoyancy of the glory-ridden,
deeper each day, into the wobbling blue.

II

Corvus

I grieved the blackbird
in his blood and smoke.

I grieved the children
who heard the blast

and saw the transformer
light up like a torch

who saw him fall
grimly from so high

as if fired out
from a homemade canon

I grieved the children
who pleaded for me

to do something
to do anything

who called out
and winced

but soon returned
to their homes

I grieved the old man
who came out to say

it will be dark
before this will be fixed

maybe midnight
before the power is restored

I grieved his old age
as he wiped his glasses

and shook his head
to release the rain

as he gazed at the wires
and bent down low

to grab a stick
and nudge the crow.

Waiting Room

I like my little corner, under a poster
of blue skies and Mt. Everest.
The kid in front of me droops
so low, it seems he's lost his head
between his knees, while his mother
moves from glowering to scowl,
as she anticipates their climb together—
glacial or volcanic, or rising from the sea.
Sometimes the mountain's no bigger
than the shallow ledge of unknowing;
or maybe it's just time slowing down,
until it sputters and stops altogether,
and one can only go forward—
through the door marked *private,*
into perilous fields of green.

Bedside Medicine

So many times I walked that long hall
only to cower outside his door, till clamor
of nurse and sick teenager subsided,
and I was invited in. Holding Russell up
became a learned art, as he slumped in every
direction, fighting back pain to generate a laugh,
while I'd languish in guilt, thinking of Kafka
and his man-turned-into-bug. Even his sister
struggled in weariness and fright against helping
the changeling. But Russell was wasting away
from the interior, and the gaunt and pale offices
of death chilled me through my teenage bones.
Looking back, I see the ravages of cancer
were his only betrayal. We were both to have
our Bar Mitzvahs on nearly the same day,
and we'd rehearsed our Torah Passages
together. But he never made it. Only days before
he passed, we squabbled over the existence
of God. Livening up, he said he never felt better,
and then collapsed backward, with one finger
pointed in my direction, calling me *Jesus*.

Henry

Grandfather on the love seat poking at us,
then turning away—nodding sideways
into guttural snoring, interrupted
by a Yiddish argument with himself.
His wife of 50 years beside him, in a rocker,
,arduously knitting another sweater.
Mom boiling tongue in the kitchen.
Earlier that day he perched me high up
on his workbench while he sorted
little metal trinkets, old bicycle spokes,
weird painted gizmos that turned and hissed.
He worked his neighborhood for junk,
sold most to his older brother who owned
a profitable company, kept the rest.
Mom calls us in, while he jabs me one last
time in the abdomen, twisting his finger
like a drill, before turning me upside down,
as I grasp for the flesh of his burning star.

This World Is Not Your Oyster

Nor your clam, nor scallop,
nor any other mollusk—
though limpet-like sea creatures
take the shape of your present mood,
with their octopus of melancholy.
When you let your guard down,
the deep black sea laps in,
and the simplest life form unhinges
its misshapen maw. This world
is not your oyster, but it may be
your best alternative, or your secret
lost treasure, an alabaster shell
whose pearl washed away
in the same winsome waves
now bearing you gently to sand.

Breakfast Chat

Grandma spoke of the Holocaust
the same way she spoke
of making eggs, lifting
the veil only once, as I waited
on a wooden chair—
the smell of rich butter
wafting my way,
thickly intoxicating—
barely cooked eggs
glistening like an omen.
She paced circles,
every other word
an unintelligible groan,
explaining how the yolk
of peace and tolerance broke.
When she finally sat down,
I learned how many had died
in the camps. And how they died.

Mashable on Twitter, 2020

I stare at a photo of a cow wading into an ocean.
The caption reads: *Cows are returning to sea,*
nature is healing. My wife puts her soft hand
on my forehead, while her free hand builds castles
of toilet paper, and masks from salvaged tee shirts—
glory days, in lieu of the nasopharyngeal swab.
She gauges the menace of Fahrenheit flow,
and spoons the last of the toffee Haagen-Dazs
to her dazzling lips, creamy as her ravishing
titanium hair. Hers is the calmness of patience,
while I stew in my own juices, a bone-house
shivering its dry cough. Which doorknob leads
to deliverance? A flowering cherry, vaccine
boosters, or the morning's soft cool breeze?
Winter's hibernation begins, but Zoom exposes
all—our kids Zooming us Zooming them.
The world's at sea, doves have nowhere to land.
Yet the handmaiden of help smiles with confidence,
moving her hand along my woolly crown. Rivers
recede, and dry land forms. *Cool as a cucumber,*
she hums, her words a slipshod courier of grace.
Earth is healing, the cows are returning to the sea.

Vinyl Lathe

Levi pointed to the inner sanctum,
his tricked-out vinyl mastering studio—
speaking of his craft not in theory
or the rubbery world of trial and error,
but raison d'être, wild-eyed oracle.
Before a record is mass-produced,
it must first be mastered on vinyl,
an iffy process balancing precision
on the edge of subjective experience.
Cutting masters on vinyl, he said,
is like juggling nitroglycerin, nudging
me closer to the disc's thin lustrous
surface, gently spinning on its bed
of air, impervious to wobble.
You can see it through a scope—thin,
nearly microscopic shards peeling away
into a loose ball, called swarf—
not a cartoon character, but dross made
from a single groove so exquisitely
formed that near-perfect music results,
a sonorous wave, from a sea of sound.

Art

Passing overhead—
hundreds of sleepy
blackbirds, pointillism
mastered in the pastel
night sky, stippling
the canvas. The sound
a monotone roar
deepening to fugue
as you dance on one foot
with a cackle and caw
like someone enfolded
in an old age spell.
And you think
the birds hear you,
and you them—
every syllable and beat
every eager flap
writing a lyrical ballad.

In the Raw

My love and I drift in the middle of a big lake,
under overcast sky, as the wind picks up.
We have no oars and the boat has no engine,
but we enjoy a lunch of tuna fish and apples,
taking turns inventing seductive story lines.
When it begins to rain, we take off our clothes
so they won't get soaked. She begins to cry,
and paddles with her hands. The shore recedes,
but I tell her we can easily swim to safety.
I belly flop in, and invite her to follow.
She leaps, and we back float until it thunders.
Can you get electrocuted in a lake, she asks,
and I tell her *no,* but she just paddles faster.
An arc of electricity bolts across the sky and lands
precisely between our two buoyant naked bodies,
transporting us back home and into our bed.
One of us lies awake, listening to the rain
pound out the *1812 Overture,* while the other
dreams of a garden, but neither of us is naked.

Pillow with Pomegranates

You pull yourself closer to a window to look
at the snowy veneer under a street lamp,

turning the surface blue. You count the birds
moving delicately from that scrim, to trees.

Isn't it like the winter to leave unwrapped gifts
at the door, surreptitiously, with strings attached?

A pile of snow, or a package loosely wrapped—
an old book, that turns out to be damaged.

What then, of the giving and the taking,
what of small loves, and larger losses?

The phone rings and rings, then stops.
Your friend from Phoenix, you guess.

Mid-morning, the freezing pane fogs
intermittently, timing measured breaths.

Both arms clasp the pillow
you should have gifted, but didn't—

red-brown pomegranates against indigo blue,
19th-century woven fabric, you were told.

Your thoughts collect in discrete bundles
like the snow, in wind-driven mounds,

the very worst of winter. Cold air pours
through an opening in the window sash,

where you place the pillow across the breach,
pressing your head against it, to stop the wind.

Shadow Passing

The jet stream floats a lone cloud,
an invisible river mapping sky,
its shadow passing overhead
like a zeppelin coming in
to cautiously land. The sky
darkens—an El Greco painting
beset by unseen warfare,
and the ancient arc of striving.
A clear path across two mountains
becomes a function of time, distance,
and inspiration's unscalable limit.
The body needs a willing mind,
but the heart is never satisfied.

Blood Farm

A large van clings to the steep unfenced canyon road,
the driver's every muscle working against its slow progress.
An inert brain wars against his lab head's directive
to collect red blood cells from the twelfth most intelligent
animal on the planet, for the first's experimental purposes.
He winds a side road and stops at a heavy gate, exits the vehicle
and squats like Cerberus guarding Hades, viewing three
older men with brows as ravens' wings wielding animal
parts like taffy, covered in the blood carcasses they slice.
Walking cautiously toward them, the taller of the three asks,
Are you Ed? He gives them a thumbs-up and a head nod,
and so begins four trips back and forth, eight sealed buckets
loaded into the back of his trunk, and the matter is settled—
Judas cash for the sake of research and development.
A large van starts traversing back down the canyon,
dust-laden air impeding its descent to the shadowed valley.
Craning forward, he reaches the relief of civilization,
village homes on lanes lit with heavenly pink trees,
dogwoods waving in a breeze bursting through car
door windows, but not enough to clear out the blood scent.

Field

Fortified by the strength of multitudes
who come to make it their home,
the tall grass need not be mown
nor lined with hedge, nor tilled.
The field will find its own dimension,
in summer's desiccating energy,
through dormancy's lulling trance.
It will house the lowly clover,
and the kingly dandelion.
It will raise proletariat grass high
toward the heavens, every June—
and by December, with little notice,
all will fade and flatten, like a carpet.

From the Rubble

Wafting eggs and bacon, clatter of sisters arguing.
Not just any Saturday, but this eight-year-old's birthday—
with a crowning present: the Seattle Totems play tonight
for the Western Hockey Championship, in Hawaii.
Adjusting time zones, three hours after bedtime,
just enough time to fill in the scorecard with players
and current stat-lines from both teams, color-coded.
Forcing myself to stay awake until gametime, I lower
the volume on my transistor radio barely loud enough
to discern the play-by-play, and discover we're down 2-0.
With the game seemingly hopeless, Guyle Fielder breaks
free and scores on a pass from the burly defenseman Sinclair,
and then another goal to tie it up. All too good to be true,
as an eerie petrichor of wet pavement filters through
an open window, wafting my way, turning into an acrid smell
of smoke, followed by Dad's shrill cries, *Fire! Fire!*
Blurred hands swoop down to grab and hurtle me out
the door, along with chairs, rugs, and the desk that held
the candle that I'd lit and set in a plastic container.
Banished to back-room confinement, I escape on all fours,
searching like a recovery dog pawing through cinders.
Charred and barely readable, I find the scorecard, still
bearing witness to the unfathomable result of a Totems'
victory, lifted from the rubble like a phoenix from ash.

Getting to the End

On a walk by the pond overshadowed by oaks,
my old dog pulls me along like a tow truck,
through a shimmering violet dusk I barely see.

I lead her to the pier's end, drawing in her harness
more and more tightly with each step,
pulling back against her press toward water.

She wears disappointment like an old cloak,
each flex and twitchy sinew a new tear,
another glittering sequin falling off.

My dog is not the dog of her youth,
romping on the tide flats in mud
up to her elbows, or wading the creek.

At fourteen, I can't let her jump in to swim.
I'm perhaps as badly worn, though less hampered,
pulling heavily on the leash, a bit crestfallen.

The long path home shortens and narrows,
as I desire more of what slips away—
forgetting what I've gained along the way.

Symphony of Broken Instruments

Star-crossed, our late and lonely planet,
forsaking the music of spheres

and those outcast in their country
of doom, noteless and bereft in rooms.

Where buoyant spirits whispered,
the doleful chorus now pours forth.

Outside, hungry bodies incarnate
requiem, street-side beds of tarpaulin

fill vaulted towers, as orchestral bells
peal their cracked, aching ballad.

Taking Inventory

I think I explored my father's side of their spacious
walk-in closet more than I explored the deep
forested ravine a few blocks away. On my mother's side
were mothballs and hats, cellophane-dressed gowns
and mounds and mounds of shoes. But my father's side
had guns and ammo, tobacco, boxes of chocolate bars
and a huge laminated treasure chest filled with silver coins.
He never caught me stealing his pistol, nor realized
I unloaded a few shells into the bark of our madrona.
He never knew I regularly reduced his supply of chocolate,
or rolled cigarettes around his musty old tobacco.
But one day he found me with every shining coin
spread out on their bed, all in rows and organized by date.
After that, the chest was sealed, a large padlock added,
and the chocolate mercilessly gone. But the luger remained
in its place on top of a box of luger bullets; and though
his story of prying it out from the hands of a dead soldier
was refuted, it still raised the hair on my boyish neck.

Petunia

Your name and face may seem mundane
to some, your color palette rarely shown
in botanical old books; but I have seen
your seeds impatient to be born,
and once breathing, never miss a breath.
I have neglected to feed and water you,
cull your dead blossoms or trim spindly excess.
Yet in this wasting season of August,
enervating any attempts at weeding—
you spill like a fountain with all your clan,
clasping hands as if to gain strength in numbers,
an army massing on the borders of my heart.

III

Nonlinear Equations for Growing Better Olives

Perhaps you've been given the grace of happy
oblivion, but I think of the stars' speed every day.
Reclining in my lawn chair pointed upward,
I see only clear blue, yet I know the stars hurtle
through space at about a half-million miles per hour
with little deflecting them but the heartthrob
of gravity. I sometimes wonder if it's me thinking
too fast, or maybe not even at all—a mere mortal
fluxed by galaxy or planet, thwarted by a tiny virus,
or rippled through by the most benign of forces.
It makes me wonder, as I dab a brow, wiping
clean the clash of unearned serendipity,
my needled imagination projecting far more
nervous doubt than the appreciation of paradox.
In forty years of biomedical research, only one
raptured dreamer ever reminded me of the simple
path, with his bench-side epithets invoking
Occam's razor, cautioning with a waving finger
and a bent smile, *Don't forget the razor!,*
while I shot the moon with complicated theories.
And now, in Seattle, my little olive trees have only
a smattering of mature ripe olives, while thousands
of shriveled, unfertilized specks dot the branches.
This is an unsolved problem I've attacked for years,
and though I'd love olives of decent size to brine
and adorn in decorated jars with custom labels,
blowing through a straw for days trying to move
pollen particles from anther to pistil takes a toll.
After explaining coronavirus and months of defending
self-evident data, taking heat for revealing obvious
conspiracy, and rubbernecking graphs and charts—
I'm left enervated, perplexed, full of survivor's guilt.
Where some see a million scattered dots, I see cytokine
storms and shining green stars birthing and dying.

A Half Calendar

Perhaps we missed
how late summer
yellowed the grasses,

or couldn't hear
the difference between
crows' or doves' wings,

but we could clench
February's snow
and brace north winds,

and we hailed March
like a prodigal friend
on the doorstep.

Along the sides
of an old barn—
a man and his dog,

and April daffodils
on their impossibly
delicate stems,

lighting up the barn's
weathered gray,
against all odds.

Chant

Wherever love is true,
God is there—
sing the monks
of Glenstal Abbey,
while I sleep in earnest.
They sing that faith
without works
is a breathless calling.
They sing as bells
ring, waking me
from their dream.
Keep your hands
free from business,
they call out,
while I write out
invoices. Let your feet
be bare, and callused,
they urge,
as slippers hug my toes.
Let your heart
pour forth like morning.

An Old Age Fable

Obligatory sagging cheeks,
red dots and gouged rivers—
your folded skin, bereft of collagen.

Not so much a map of destination,
or leaving home; not even the angst
of slowing down, or losing grip.

If you gangster the mirror,
features less ominous may appear,
a cryptograph, or algorithm.

Once upon a time, the barred owl's
soothing *Who's who* magicked you
rhythmically back to sleep,

but these days a predatory heartbeat
stalks your forested pathways,
a chink in the armor of commonplace—

opening highways to clearer fields,
green glades ghosted
by the sleek animal of youth.

The Zero Hour

Thursday carried an osmium weight
of things unfinished—hours slinking
off like a lost cat, gone beyond hunger.

You were feeling sluggish, but at your age,
with wellness being an unattainable goal,
your unflagging spirit was an unexpected gift.

And we were slogging through long hours,
tasked to sort family treasures from common
clutter, busy all day culling and saving—

additions and subtractions, a null set
of missed opportunity, as you prepared
to take your own soundless departure.

We guided you into bed, lifting your shoulders
to help the long air of relief push through,
a last sigh fleeting from your pressed lips.

Algorithms for Bisecting a Polygon

I heard that you can stand in a vat of cornstarch
and water, if the concentrations and ratios are right,
and you can prance on its meniscus without sinking
an inch, thanks to the rheology of suspensions.
And if you bisect the interior angles of a polygon,
the bisectors will always converge in the polygon's
incenter—not really centered anywhere but the wide,
ineffable world of mathematics. Solar systems
and the flux of atoms are based on geometry,
but seldom linear; and red sky at night does not
always make sailors delight, a sad fact for vacationers.
As I scan one of Einstein's biographies, I see that light
of any color travels at the same 300,000 km per second,
but bends measurably when it gets near heavenly bodies
or cosmic holes. And though understanding mystery
doesn't require mastering calculus, the dog at my feet
barks every time I turn the page, a synchronicity
corresponding to the blasts of a nearby car alarm.
Here is geometry's epicenter and the ascendancy
of stars—exact moments of clarity seemingly fading
away, then coalescing in crescendo, and with them,
the weight of having to bear it, mercifully lifted.

Rarified Air

A fly at the cusp of a wine glass,
a little buzz shared, interspecies.
Chateau Margaux, or a wine cooler—
the soul rattling from phylum to phylum,
eager to step into the vast blue-gray.
I once heard a fly sees tens of thousands
of different patterns spread out evenly
like wildflowers across its visual field.
Imagine the dreams thus wrought,
after all that flitting, landing in soft
clover, at dusk. Go ahead, dream
the world dancing, prismatic.
Imagine a fly's dalliance as elegant
as your own sweet dreamscape,
an argument sublime enough
to account for the littlest wing,
the smallest vacuole of concern.
Or, whisk it away like dust.
Not the dream, but the fly, I mean.

Boys of Summer

I never got out of boxers today.
Do I have to make excuses?
I track the early evening's moon
with a carnal eye, tempt fates
with an irresistible urge to howl.
What can be said of a body
set in motion, that tends to stay
at rest, integral of E to the X power?
These shooting pains of mortality—
a full year's supply of ennui,
and I've barely made it to April.
Are we meant to creep about
the house as wrinkled bodies,
concaved into the sofa's crevice?
The first baseball game arrives
today, coronavirus be damned—
under the lights of an Eastern sky,
without a partisan in the stands.
We shelter-in-place electronically,
through wired portals, under lavish
sunsets and the burgeoning dusk.
I open a beer and fetch some nuts,
as the mighty Yankees take the field,
and the Red Sox prepare to bat.
The players have all been tested,
but we're in limbo land, hunkered
in stuffy rooms, preoccupied—staring
down a tall left-hander in pinstripes,
just looking for a good pitch to hit.

Dance of Deception

A harbinger crow just landed on my deck,
so I know my left hip's going to be a problem—
and don't forget the final caw of death and dying.
I should try and forget, as we make our dusky way
through gruyere and crusted bread, dotted
with fig jam, and a fine red wine in the offing.
But the crow's proprioception is more boundless
than my patience, pacing like a surveyor,
hopping on one leg, and now balancing atop
the chimney like a gymnast. He has bad manners,
eager to disrupt the harmony of my evening.
As my love sighs nearby in angel breaths that soothe,
I grunt and groan in a familiar, yet unknown tongue.

Threnody

A door propped slightly ajar
by coincidence or celestial hint,
breaths away from breaching darkness.
Have you discerned such a space,
or imagined a room inhabiting its void?
Is there a place so remote and desolate,
you wouldn't venture its discovery?
A narrow slant of light might draw you
to its nuanced shelter, raying
your shadowed footsteps, or maybe
it's the dark cavern that calls you,
with its promise of sheltered gloom.
In the grinding cogs of industry,
perhaps a small glimpse of your own
diminishing has brought you closer
to a foothold, no matter how far
the mind wanders free from the body.

Ocarina

I keep singing to my father the same song
he'd sing to me, belching uproariously,
waggling his teaching finger by my eyes,
It's not what you do, it's how you do it—
and though he's long gone, I keep singing
of the way he taught me to laugh, to *own it,*
with a body rumbling from the pain.

My father found his second calling
in learning to play the ocarina.
Invented twelve thousand years ago,
the stubby little wooden flute sounded
like ancient tribes summoning their gods,
but resembled a modern blow dryer
we kids would swipe to mock-dry our hair.
He'd play it as we ate or watched TV,
adding trills and accents to elicit a laugh.

He'd even play it driving the car—
his only son egging him on, until Mom
tried to pull it away: *You'll kill us all!*
But he played on, fishtailing the freeway,
with his knees propped up to steer,
all three kids in the back, belly laughing.
Today, I go him one better, playing the flute
I palmed after his funeral, attempting the tune
he used to sing me, as I float down my own
road, steering with the sinew of memory.

Dream Sequence

I feel again my mentor's breath
who enjoyed hovering over me in the lab
rubbing his thumbs together like Boris Karloff
morbidly declaring that apoptosis is not death
but an illuminating message for biologists
with its dead ringer onomatopoeia
and threat of programmed cell death
all sequenced in the backbone of a DNA helix.
Mixed with layering thickets of dream
I am further harassed by a plump lime
that's just fallen on me from a potted tree.
Angels of lucidity attempt to entrance me
through a closed window as monkeys
type out an entire Encyclopedia Britannica
including a 30-page treatise describing citrus
with color aquatints. My shoulder throbs
not from the lime but the sudden ribosomal
hijacking of deltoid muscle as new defenses
mount their hidden wings. Honeysuckle wafts
through my window. Spring in counterforce.
Songbirds and bees. The smell of damp earth
and the drumming rain stunning me awake.

The Solitary Yoshino Cherry Tree

I water the cherry tree late in summer
as drought threatens; and in early March,
I get all the blossoms one man can handle.

I cook the pancakes, but you make the batter.
I remember to get the ducks up,
feed the dog and administer her medicine.

But you remember and remind me, tomorrow
is the anniversary of your mother's birth,
and that your grandmother died the same day,

two days shy of her twenty-second leap year.
You remember baking your mom
a yellow birthday cake with raspberry jam,

and sticking it in the cupboard—
but after your grandmother's funeral,
you found it molded beyond recognition.

This year, the cherry tree lost its blossoms
after only two weeks, from excess rain
and wind, though it was probably my fault—

partly from neglect, though I remembered
to photograph it when it was in full bloom,
and I remembered to send it to my friends.

But you remind me how your grandfather
remained active, practicing medicine
nearly up until his death in his nineties—

how he spent the hour after his wife's death
trying to give her breath, long after a doctor
of his stature must have known she was gone.

Death's Apprentice

He doesn't like his work any more than you do—
out the door at dawn, hoping to retire by midnight,
dragged from bed by the inevitable 2am house call.
He'd much rather spend his nights in dusky clubs,
singing the blues and plucking his bass, or sitting
on a couch for weeks on end, watching *Friends*.
But Death continues to support his deadbeat family,
trying to keep up with more chic grim reapers—
lying awake dreaming of the Greek Island cottage
he got for a song, but so far, has never visited.
Now, as homo sapiens over-populate, draining
dregs from the world's urn, he feels more urgency
to serve, to meet the ultimate need, stoically—
his somber but earnest public face haunting shadows,
knifing the air with his bluesy riff—as the train he steers
dopplers through each station, stopping on a moment's
soft breath, to collect the next unwilling passenger.

Over the Threshold

The month I dread most is the one now upon me,
October's ghost wind rattling branches, turning ochre
the sodden leaf mold, eerily weeping worms.
October is the month which now delivers solace,
a cruel replacement for the sorrow of losing a pet—
sending its half-moon shroud to enfold, its unseen
microbial kingdom, to foment. We must creep through
darkness to achieve a deeper healing—breathing ancient
atoms where the dead abide and prosper, bringing back
into view this fleeting beauty. A motley funeral
procession of ghouls and pumpkins now line the roads
we used to walk; ground now hallowed in memory.
Sofie couldn't step out of the van, so we lifted
and set her gently down, where she remained steady
on all four feet, as the vet came out to meet her.
But she wouldn't advance, until I moved slowly
toward the door, hearing her shuffle behind—
one leg turning up and dragging on the pavement,
and then the next, as she followed me across the threshold
of another adventure, into the brilliance of her beyond.

The Kindness of Rivers

If a river runs through heaven,
I've not heard its name

but I've fancied I could describe
its length and breadth.

Not the river named Pain
nor Wailing—nor Senescence

whose sad folk gather at its side
without swim suits or picnic baskets.

I used to think I'd like to be buried
in its steep and narrow valley

chiseled by the lazy flow of centuries,
its silt laid down atom by atom.

I would admire the sheen of pools,
home to herons and fingerlings

imploring me to slow down,
dip my aching feet in its soothing chill.

I used to imagine my progeny there
and their progeny as well,

multitudinous in their fine array,
reconvening every August

to dance on its pebbled shores
thinking of nothing special

but the old river's youthful cry
pouring effortlessly out.

The Inevitable Practicality of Water

And what might this world have looked like,
without the hydrogen bond? Perhaps an airy
sea of stones, something dry and shifty
washing my skin; a cloudless sky, or an empty
pond where blue heron maneuver to mate,
their chalky paws not webbed, but calloused.
Gone the splash and marauder of youthful feet;
gone quench, sheen, mercurial touch, buoyancy.
Vanished at dusk, all reds and pinks off water's
edge, the lapping sound, salt it brings to your nose.
Gone summer steam off blacktop, winter solid.
The snow never heaped on sidewalks nor collected
along streets in Boston—those burly blokes wielding
plows attached to their four-by-fours never
patrolled side streets with their keen, altruistic eyes.
Desiccated earthlings never learned the mystery
in all three phases, compacted, boiling, pouring
back into drains, back to brackish shores
or passing through sky's gritty filter and returning
pure as the cottony snow. Nowhere to be seen,
an ice cube, cumulonimbus, a slipping tear.

Blanket of Subtlety

I spent a day wandering in and out
of my thoughts, the way a child
tents a blanket with chairs to crawl
its dim recesses—beginning early
with soft light breaking through
a sliver opening in the curtains,
as a summer wind might sieve
a tree, its soft rattling
barely noticeable, until it is.
When sibilance turns from hissing
snakes, to rustling leaves, or distant
airplanes barely audible.
Falling asleep, bamboo scrapes
a partially shuttered window
strobing the street lamp
with intervals of noise and music,
alto and soprano, vibrato—
the heat and the light and the sound.

A New Theory of Time

The star-studded universe mocks an arrow's arc,
rocketing sideways through a vacuum from our here
and now in spacetime units, out to the faraway of matter
and motion. Einstein said that past, present and future
merge, hermetically sealed in an airless chamber.
Today, at MIT, we hear elaboration, after a century
of time travel and sci-fi lure—more solidly fixed we are,
they tell us, diverted only temporarily from vanishing,
in a static hole the universe accelerator ignores.
We can't go back to stop a fire or divert a flood,
there's no teleporting from pandemic to future cure.
The table's set, the lights are low, and fine linen
has been delicately laid—red wine brims the glass
we lift, to savor and herald, every tannic drop.

In Lieu of Sheep

Last night, to convince
myself to sleep, a version
of a younger me appeared
with its algorithm
of relief, a simple game
of doubling numbers,
until soft and warm,
the fluff of numbness
pressed my head
into the pillow
lulling me senseless
with its clever sleight
of hand. 2-4-8-16-32 . . .
a geometric sequence
as challenging as it is
dumbing to the senses.
I could see and hear
my youthful nemesis,
dancing at the edge of
a galaxy, more remote
than Pascal's Triangle.
Four billion, two-hundred
and ninety-four million,
nine-hundred and sixty-
seven thousand, two-
hundred and ninety-six.
Two, to the thirty-second
power of lucid dreaming.

Secondary Effects

I could say the warm afterglow
of meeting you in the park
carried me like a swing,
your sun-drenched tresses
brightening the air, the proximal
benefit of companionship
broadening into a riot of joy
amid the exalted murmur
of ocean spray and waterfowl.
I could add that the result
thwarted all ills and tiny rifts
in our life's short breath,
a mending of worldly disorder.
But, walking the wind-swept shore,
your hand wrapping my elbow's
crook, and your blinking eyes
fighting back tears of relief,
companioned a far greater
transfiguration. Sand underfoot,
a dying sun reborn through clouds,
the unexplainable urge to laugh—
our toes dipping playfully
into the surging tide of our time.

About the Author

Edward Nudelman's full-length poetry collections include: *Thin Places* (Salmon Poetry, forthcoming, 2024); *Out of Time, Running* (Harbor Mountain, 2014); *What Looks Like an Elephant* (Lummox, 2011); and *Night Fires* (Pudding House, 2009). Poems have appeared in *Rattle, Cortland Review, Valparaiso Review, Chiron Review, Evergreen Review, Floating Bridge, Plainsongs, Penwood Review, Poets and Artists,* and many more. Awards include: finalist in 2019 Atlanta Review International Poetry Contest (two poems), honorable mention in 2019 Passager Poetry Contest, second place for the Indie Lit Awards Book of the Year (*What Looks Like an Elephant*), semifinalist for the Journal Award, OSU Press (*Night Fires*), and a Pushcart nomination.

A native Seattleite, Nudelman is a recently retired cancer research scientist, and owns/operates a rare bookshop (est. 1980) where he lives in Seattle, with his wife, dog, and five ducks.

Made in United States
Troutdale, OR
11/08/2023